M4 MacBook Pro

A Story of Innovation, Performance, and Vision

An Analytical Journey into Apple's Latest Laptop – EVERYTHING YOU NEED TO KNOW

Joe E. Grayson

Outline

Introduction

As anticipation built to a fever pitch, tech enthusiasts and professionals alike waited with bated breath for Apple's latest leap forward: the unveiling of the MacBook Pro equipped with the highly anticipated M4 series. Apple has long been recognized as a visionary force in technology, consistently setting standards that others aspire to match, yet rarely do. Its influence goes far beyond crafting sleek, stylish devices. Over the years, Apple has redefined user experience, shaping the way people interact with technology in ways that go unnoticed until, suddenly, they're indispensable. Every MacBook Pro iteration has pushed the envelope, each release generating waves of excitement as consumers, industry leaders, and creatives look forward to the next revolutionary upgrade that promises to change how they work, create, and explore.

The release of the M4 series has marked yet another chapter in this ongoing saga. For those familiar with Apple's in-house chip journey, this series was more than just another upgrade; it symbolized a new horizon in computing performance and efficiency. When Apple first introduced its custom silicon, the M1, it was heralded as a game changer, shifting expectations for power, speed, and versatility. Now, with the M4 series, Apple once again dares to challenge and evolve those standards, infusing this model with enhancements meant to tackle the demands of a constantly advancing digital landscape. But beyond mere performance metrics, the M4 series represents something even more ambitious: a vision for what portable computing could, and perhaps should, be.

This book invites readers to step into a world where performance, innovation, and aesthetic merge seamlessly. With an analytical lens paired with a storytelling approach, it delves deep into the MacBook Pro's design, functionality, and unique appeal, providing insights not just for tech aficionados but also for those who might be deciding on their next investment. Whether you're a creative professional, a curious tech enthusiast, or simply someone intrigued by Apple's technological journey, this exploration will offer you an enriched perspective on why the M4 series MacBook Pro has captured so much attention. The chapters to follow aim to unpack the features that set it apart, the intricate balance of power and efficiency that defines it, and the lasting impact it may have on the industry and its users.

Chapter 1: The Evolution of the MacBook Pro

The MacBook Pro's story began as a testament to Apple's relentless pursuit of pushing computing boundaries, capturing attention for both its design and capability. When first launched, it set itself apart as a powerful tool crafted to meet the demands of professionals who relied on performance, speed, and precision. From photographers and videographers to software developers and scientists, the MacBook Pro became an essential tool, trusted for its ability to handle complex tasks without compromising on elegance. For years, these machines were powered by Intel chips, delivering robust performance yet always hinting at an untapped potential just beneath the surface, waiting to be unlocked.

Each generation of the MacBook Pro refined this potential, introducing innovative changes and setting new industry benchmarks. Milestones like the introduction of the Retina display, which brought stunning clarity and color accuracy, or the inclusion of the Touch Bar, redefined interactivity and usability. Then came advancements in keyboard design, trackpad sensitivity, and a steady evolution toward slimmer profiles that balanced portability with the power that users expected. Yet, even with these developments, a sense of limitation persisted—especially as Apple began envisioning a future where they could control not just the design but also the very heart of their machines: the processing chip itself.

This ambition materialized in the form of Apple Silicon, a major pivot in Apple's technological journey. The first M1 chip, launched in 2020, was not just an update but a bold reimagining of what Apple's computers could achieve. With an integrated design that allowed for enhanced performance and energy efficiency, the M1 was Apple's first statement of independence from third-party processors, and the results were staggering. The new chip brought performance gains that seemed almost inconceivable, allowing even the most compact MacBook models to outperform their previous Intel-powered predecessors. With its seamless blend of CPU, GPU, and neural engine, the M1 opened the door to an era of optimized software-hardware synergy that Apple alone could control. This success story continued with the M2 and M3 series, each iteration refining Apple's vision and establishing the MacBook Pro as the go-to tool for professional users.

Now, with the introduction of the M4, Apple has once again elevated the MacBook Pro's standing in the world of computing. As part of Apple's roadmap for its silicon family, the M4 serves as the pinnacle of their engineering so far, harnessing advanced 3-nanometer architecture to deliver unprecedented speed, power efficiency, and graphics capability. By integrating all these elements under Apple's control, the M4 series represents a major leap forward in performance, catering specifically to the needs of users who demand the best. Creative professionals working in 4K video editing, 3D rendering, or graphic design can now rely on a laptop that not only matches but often exceeds the capabilities of desktop setups, all in a portable form. Meanwhile, everyday users benefit from a more fluid experience, faster app processing, and battery efficiency that makes a day without a charger a viable reality.

In this evolution, the MacBook Pro with the M4 series stands as a testament to Apple's promise to marry form and function in ways that meet diverse needs. Whether for intense professional use or as a premium everyday device, this model promises to deliver on every front, pushing the MacBook Pro into a new era that speaks to the heart of Apple's philosophy: the seamless integration of innovation, performance, and vision.

Chapter 2: The Heart of the Machine – The M4 Chip

At the core of Apple's latest MacBook Pro is the groundbreaking M4 chip, marking a new pinnacle in Apple's silicon journey. This series comprises three distinct variations tailored to different levels of professional and personal use: the M4, M4 Pro, and M4 Max. Each version builds on the last, scaling power and efficiency in ways that allow users to choose a model that best suits their needs, whether for demanding creative tasks, complex data analysis, or simply a seamless day-to-day experience.

The base M4 chip is designed for users who need robust, reliable performance with a significant boost over prior models. It offers impressive speed for most applications, including intensive multitasking, light video editing, and handling high-resolution media with ease. For those who require greater horsepower, the M4 Pro delivers an elevated performance tier, allowing smooth processing for activities like 4K video editing, photo manipulation, and complex rendering. At the top of the range, the M4 Max stands as Apple's ultimate chip, geared towards users with specialized, high-performance needs. Ideal for 3D rendering, advanced gaming development, or machine learning tasks, this chip brings unparalleled power and flexibility in a portable form. Each of these options offers users a degree of customization, empowering them to match their tools to the demands of their work and lifestyle.

Underlying these variations is Apple's leap to a 3-nanometer chip architecture, a sophisticated engineering feat that improves processing power, efficiency, and thermal management. This technology allows more transistors to fit within the chip, leading to higher CPU and GPU performance without compromising energy efficiency. The CPU itself is structured with high-performance cores balanced by energy-efficient cores, resulting in a powerful yet balanced engine capable of handling a wide array of tasks. GPU improvements allow for faster graphics processing, making tasks like video rendering and gaming more fluid and visually rich. Additionally, the neural engine within the M4 family has been expanded to support more intensive AI-driven tasks, from machine learning algorithms to real-time image and video enhancements.

Battery life is one of the most celebrated achievements of the M4 chip lineup, where efficiency has been carefully optimized to extend usage without frequent charging. With each chip variant, users experience gains in battery longevity—an invaluable feature, especially in high-performance machines. The M4 base model's battery is designed to sustain typical workdays, while the Pro and Max versions offer extended power cycles even under heavy loads. These energy improvements allow users to experience the full capability of their MacBook Pro throughout the day without sacrificing performance or reaching for a charger.

In terms of processing power, the M4 series represents a remarkable evolution from its predecessors. Compared to the M1, M2, and M3, the M4 chip offers substantial improvements in CPU speed, AI processing, and GPU performance, making it a formidable tool in every benchmark. In particular, AI and graphics performance have been pushed to new limits. For creative professionals, the advancements in real-time rendering and media processing mean smoother workflows and faster exports. In areas such as data science and engineering, the M4 Max provides capabilities that handle simulation and modeling work more efficiently than ever before.

The M4 series stands as a robust foundation for the MacBook Pro's design, delivering a spectrum of power and versatility across its three variations. Whether users require advanced performance for specialized tasks or reliable power for everyday needs, the M4 chip family transforms the MacBook Pro into a machine that can adapt to any challenge while staying energy-efficient and portable, embodying Apple's vision of uncompromised performance in every sense.

Chapter 3: Display – Visuals That Captivate

The MacBook Pro's display has long been one of its most celebrated features, and with the M4 series, Apple has raised the bar even higher, delivering visuals that captivate and immerse users in their work. Among the most noteworthy additions is the Nano-Texture display option, a technology that transforms the viewing experience by minimizing glare and reflections. This specialized nano-texturing, applied directly to the glass, diffuses light to prevent disruptive reflections, making it ideal for professionals working in various lighting conditions. Whether used under bright studio lights or in outdoor environments, the Nano-Texture display ensures that visuals remain crisp and clear, allowing users to focus on their content rather than adjusting for ambient light.

The brilliance of the M4 series display doesn't stop at anti-reflective properties. Apple has enhanced both Standard Dynamic Range (SDR) and High Dynamic Range (HDR) brightness levels, pushing SDR brightness to an impressive 1,000 nits and HDR up to a peak of 1,600 nits. This increase means that everyday usage, from browsing to professional editing, is sharper, brighter, and more vivid, making colors pop and details stand out even in well-lit environments. For users working with HDR content, these brightness levels allow for precise color grading and a more accurate representation of the final product. Paired with the display's 120 Hz refresh rate, which provides smooth motion and fluid responsiveness, the MacBook Pro's screen truly shines. The higher refresh rate is especially noticeable when scrolling, gaming, or editing video, creating a seamless experience that brings each frame to life with precision and smoothness.

Beneath these enhancements lies Apple's commitment to Mini-LED technology, a significant factor in achieving such high brightness levels and color fidelity. Unlike traditional LED displays, which rely on larger backlight zones, Mini-LED technology uses thousands of tiny LEDs for more localized backlight control, resulting in deeper blacks and greater contrast. This improvement has allowed Apple to deliver HDR content with stunning accuracy, making the display a strong contender for professional-grade media creation. However, there is a growing conversation around OLED technology, which is well-regarded for its true blacks and contrast, qualities that stem from

OLED's self-emissive pixels that don't require backlighting.

While OLED offers certain advantages in contrast, especially in dark environments, Mini-LED's higher brightness levels make it a more versatile choice for users who need both clarity in bright settings and color accuracy for media work. Mini-LED displays are also less prone to screen burn-in, an issue that can sometimes affect OLED screens over time. For those looking for a balance of peak brightness, color accuracy, and longevity, Mini-LED remains a compelling option, though the potential for OLED in future MacBook models keeps the conversation alive.

Together, these advancements in the M4 series MacBook Pro's display showcase Apple's dedication to delivering a visually rich, high-performance experience. From the glare-reducing Nano-Texture option to the amplified brightness and fluid refresh rate, the display is crafted to meet the needs of professionals and general users alike, immersing them in a world of sharpness, depth, and clarity that brings any project to life.

Chapter 4: Power and Battery Life

One of the standout features of the MacBook Pro with the M4 series is its exceptional battery life, a result of Apple's relentless pursuit of efficiency without sacrificing performance. This iteration promises up to 24 hours of life on a single charge, marking a substantial improvement that extends the laptop's usability throughout an entire day and beyond. Apple has fine-tuned its approach to power management, integrating advancements in battery chemistry with intelligent software algorithms that balance energy use according to task intensity. This means that whether you're browsing the web, working on documents, or taking a break to stream video content, the battery adapts seamlessly, delivering maximum efficiency across a range of tasks.

In everyday use, the battery life truly shines. Regular activities like browsing, document editing, and moderate multitasking place minimal strain on the system, allowing the battery to last close to its full potential. For more demanding tasks, such as video editing or gaming, the battery performance remains impressive. While these intensive processes do require more power, the M4 architecture efficiently manages energy consumption to prolong battery life, ensuring that creators and gamers alike experience fewer interruptions. This means that whether you're rendering high-resolution video on Final Cut Pro or playing graphics-intensive games, the MacBook Pro's battery can handle extended sessions without tethering you to a power source.

Central to these gains in battery performance is the M4 chip's architecture, which has been carefully crafted for energy efficiency at every level. Apple's 3-nanometer technology allows for higher performance per watt, meaning the chip can perform more tasks with less energy, effectively maximizing both speed and battery life. By balancing high-performance and energy-efficient cores, the M4 ensures that simpler tasks draw minimal power while saving the heavy lifting for moments when it's truly needed. This intelligent distribution of power enables the MacBook Pro to maintain its peak performance without quickly depleting its battery, an advantage that gives users on the go the freedom to work or create for hours on end without constantly checking the battery indicator.

For those who travel frequently or rely on their MacBook Pro as a primary workstation, this balance of power and efficiency brings practical, tangible benefits. Gone are the days of searching for an outlet in a crowded coffee shop or airport terminal. The MacBook Pro with the M4 chip is designed to keep pace with a fast-moving lifestyle, ready to support users through lengthy projects, travel days, or late-night creative sessions. This combination of power and battery life not only reflects Apple's engineering prowess but also aligns with the core needs of modern users, proving that high performance and energy efficiency can coexist harmoniously in a single, portable machine.

Chapter 5: Ports and Connectivity

The MacBook Pro's ports and connectivity options have always been central to its appeal, designed to support an array of devices and workflows without compromising the laptop's sleek design. In this latest iteration, Apple has introduced Thunderbolt 5 on models equipped with the M4 Pro and M4 Max chips, a decision that firmly anchors these laptops in a future-ready position. Thunderbolt 5 provides substantial bandwidth improvements over its predecessor, allowing for faster data transfers, enhanced display support, and compatibility with high-performance docks and external storage options. This added power is particularly useful for professionals working with large files or complex data, as it reduces wait times and improves overall workflow efficiency. Additionally, Thunderbolt 5's robust connectivity prepares users for future peripherals, making it a sound investment for those planning to keep their MacBook Pro as their primary machine for years to come.

Apple has also made strategic updates to the MacBook Pro's physical ports, adding a third Thunderbolt port to the 14-inch model. This added flexibility means users now have greater freedom to connect multiple displays or high-speed peripherals without relying on external adapters. For many users, especially those using the base MacBook Pro model, this enhancement transforms their setup possibilities, supporting up to two external displays along with the laptop's primary screen. This expanded capability is particularly valuable for multitasking professionals who need additional screen real estate for tasks like video editing, coding, or large-scale project management.

Complementing these upgrades is the support for Wi-Fi 6E, which brings faster and more reliable wireless connectivity, especially in crowded network environments. Wi-Fi 6E extends Wi-Fi 6 capabilities into the 6 GHz band, which reduces interference from other devices and allows for higher speeds and lower latency. This improvement translates into a smoother online experience, from faster download speeds to more stable video calls, an essential feature for remote workers and creators sharing large files across the cloud. While Apple has not yet integrated Wi-Fi 7, which is still in its early stages of adoption, Wi-Fi 6E offers a powerful, stable solution that meets the needs of most users today.

Altogether, these connectivity advancements in the M4 series MacBook Pro offer users a more versatile, future-proofed setup. Thunderbolt 5, expanded port options, and the inclusion of Wi-Fi 6E not only enhance performance but also cater to a diverse range of professional needs, ensuring that this laptop remains a reliable and adaptable tool in an increasingly connected world. For users prioritizing both functionality and adaptability, the MacBook Pro's upgraded ports and connectivity options make it well-suited for today's workflows and tomorrow's innovations.

Chapter 6: Camera, Center Stage, and Beyond

In today's world, where virtual interactions have become an integral part of both professional and personal lives, Apple has recognized the importance of a high-quality camera experience in the MacBook Pro. The latest M4 series model is equipped with an upgraded 12 MP webcam that delivers sharp, clear visuals even in varying lighting conditions, ensuring users look their best on every call. This upgrade is particularly valuable for remote workers, students, and creatives who rely on video communication to connect and collaborate across distances. Whether you're joining a virtual meeting or recording content for your audience, the enhanced camera quality provides a more polished and professional presence.

A standout feature of this new webcam is Apple's Center Stage, which intelligently adjusts the frame to keep users centered as they move. Originally introduced in the iPad, Center Stage brings dynamic framing to the MacBook Pro, following the subject as they shift or turn, creating a natural and engaging video experience. This is especially useful for presenters, teachers, and content creators who may move around during presentations or demonstrations. Instead of remaining static, the camera anticipates movement and responds fluidly, giving users the freedom to engage more naturally with their audience. For collaborative settings, whether during a creative brainstorming session or a virtual family gathering, Center Stage ensures that the focus remains where it should be, without needing constant manual adjustment.

Apple's upgrades to the MacBook Pro's camera aren't limited to visuals; they've also enhanced the audio experience. The new setup is designed to deliver richer sound quality and a more immersive audio-visual experience, crucial for users in professional settings where clarity is paramount. Improved video and audio quality means fewer distractions, making virtual interactions feel as close to in-person as possible. For users creating digital content, the enhanced setup allows for high-quality, on-the-go recording directly from the laptop, eliminating the need for external equipment in many scenarios.

Altogether, the MacBook Pro's camera and audio improvements reflect Apple's understanding of today's interconnected world, where strong visuals and sound are no longer optional but essential. The 12 MP webcam and Center Stage feature create a seamless, polished video experience, while high-quality audio ensures that every conversation, meeting, and recording sounds as good as it looks. This integration of advanced video and audio technology empowers users to engage with confidence, whether in casual calls or high-stakes professional environments, making the MacBook Pro a versatile tool in the age of virtual connection.

Chapter 7: Core Features and Configurations

The MacBook Pro with the M4 series introduces key upgrades to memory and storage, aligning with the demands of today's users and their increasingly complex workflows. The base configuration now starts with 16 GB of memory and 512 GB of storage, a significant improvement that caters to professionals and casual users alike. In a world where multitasking is the norm, 16 GB of memory provides enough power for users to seamlessly switch between tasks, run multiple applications, and handle intensive processes without slowing down. For everyday tasks such as browsing, document editing, and media consumption, this setup offers ample speed and storage, making it an ideal choice for those seeking reliable performance without extra cost.

For users with more demanding needs, Apple offers high-end configurations that take the MacBook Pro's capabilities to the next level. The M4 Max 16-inch model is designed for professionals working in fields that require maximum computing power and expansive storage. Equipped with up to 128 GB of memory and a staggering 8 TB of storage, this top-tier configuration is ideal for creators and engineers managing large files, complex data sets, or high-resolution media. Video editors, game developers, and designers can benefit immensely from this setup, as it allows for real-time rendering, 3D modeling, and other resource-intensive tasks that demand both speed and capacity. The M4 Max provides an unparalleled workspace, freeing users from the need for external storage or additional processing power and empowering them to push their creative boundaries.

Apple's pricing structure reflects the variety of configurations available, allowing users to choose models that match their specific needs and budget. The base 14-inch MacBook Pro, equipped with the standard M4 chip, 16 GB of memory, and 512 GB of storage, offers an accessible entry point for those seeking a powerful yet affordable machine. For users who require more than what the base model offers, the M4 Pro and M4 Max configurations are available, with additional costs tied to their enhanced capabilities. Moving to a 16-inch display or upgrading to the M4 Pro or Max naturally raises the price, reflecting the increase in power, memory, and storage.

In terms of value, each model presents a distinct cost-benefit proposition. The base configuration is ideal for most users, providing an efficient blend of power and affordability that suits general needs without overloading on extras. The mid-tier M4 Pro configuration offers substantial upgrades in memory and speed, making it suitable for users who work in professional software environments, need multi-display support, or run more intensive applications. Meanwhile, the M4 Max represents the pinnacle of the MacBook Pro lineup, crafted for those whose work requires nothing short of the best in computing power. For high-budget buyers and organizations, this model is a long-term investment in peak performance.

Apple has carefully calibrated each configuration to serve different user types, from casual consumers to top-tier professionals, making the

MacBook Pro with the M4 series as versatile as it is powerful. Each model offers distinct value, allowing users to choose the balance of memory, storage, and processing power that best aligns with their ambitions and workflows. This thoughtful range of options reflects Apple's commitment to meeting modern demands while delivering a device that stands the test of time.

Chapter 8: Design, Aesthetics, and Build Quality

Apple's design philosophy has long centered around the harmonious blend of elegance and functionality, a vision that continues with the latest MacBook Pro models in the M4 series. This laptop is crafted to be more than just a powerful machine; it's a refined instrument designed to meet the demands of professional and personal use while maintaining Apple's signature aesthetic. Every contour and detail is meticulously thought out, ensuring that the device is as visually appealing as it is practical. The streamlined, minimalist appearance reflects Apple's commitment to timeless design, steering clear of unnecessary embellishments while emphasizing clean lines and a sophisticated finish that appeals to users who value both form and function.

One noticeable update in the MacBook Pro's look is Apple's decision to phase out the Space Gray color, a mainstay for many years, and replace it with Space Black across all models. This new color option gives the MacBook Pro a sleek, polished appearance that exudes professionalism and durability. The deep black finish not only resists fingerprints and smudges but also aligns well with the MacBook Pro's premium positioning in Apple's lineup, giving it an unmistakable presence. Additionally, the device's aluminum enclosure provides a lightweight yet robust structure, offering resilience against daily wear and tear while keeping the device cool and comfortable to use.

Apple has also carefully considered the practical side of portability with these models. The MacBook Pro is available in two sizes: the compact, lighter 14-inch model and the larger, more expansive 16-inch version. The 14-inch option strikes a balance between performance and portability, making it ideal for users who need to travel or move frequently but still require a high-performance machine. The 16-inch model, while slightly heavier, offers a broader canvas that is invaluable for users in fields like design, media production, and software development, where screen space can significantly impact productivity. Both sizes maintain a thin profile, keeping the laptops easy to carry without sacrificing performance.

In essence, the MacBook Pro's design choices reflect Apple's dedication to meeting the diverse needs of its user base. By focusing on functional beauty, durable materials, and balanced dimensions, Apple has created a device that doesn't just perform at the highest levels but also embodies a refined aesthetic. Whether users opt for the compact 14-inch model or the expansive 16-inch version, they're investing in a machine that combines cutting-edge technology with an enduring sense of style. This attention to design and build quality ensures that the MacBook Pro remains a statement of Apple's commitment to excellence, providing users with a laptop that is as much a pleasure to hold and use as it is a powerhouse of productivity.

Chapter 9: The Role of Apple Intelligence

Apple Intelligence represents a major step forward in how Apple integrates machine learning and artificial intelligence directly into its devices, allowing users to experience enhanced, seamless interactions that go beyond simple computing power. This suite of AI-driven capabilities is embedded into Apple's silicon, utilizing specialized cores within the M4 chip to perform complex calculations and adaptations in real time. These features go far beyond standard performance enhancements—they are designed to adapt to user habits, streamline processes, and support a more intuitive interaction with technology. By leveraging Apple Intelligence, the MacBook Pro becomes not just a tool but a responsive assistant that learns and evolves based on individual usage patterns.

In practical terms, Apple Intelligence manifests in various applications that significantly improve productivity and multitasking. For example, AI algorithms help optimize battery life by analyzing typical usage patterns and adjusting power consumption based on the user's needs. Machine learning tasks, from facial recognition in photo libraries to predictive text in typing, benefit from Apple Intelligence's advanced neural processing, which is built directly into the hardware. This integration allows for rapid, secure processing of data without relying on external servers, ensuring both speed and privacy. For professionals, Apple Intelligence can streamline workflows, suggesting files and applications that users frequently access and predicting next steps, saving time across repetitive tasks.

The potential applications of Apple Intelligence extend beyond what's currently available, hinting at a future where the MacBook Pro could become even more adaptive and proactive in its functions. With advancements in machine learning, Apple Intelligence could evolve to support increasingly sophisticated tasks, from real-time language translation to predictive task management that adapts to user schedules and workflows. As AI technology progresses, Apple may continue to expand the capabilities of its neural engines, making each iteration of Apple Silicon smarter and more capable. The groundwork laid by Apple Intelligence hints at a long-term vision where the MacBook Pro—and potentially other Apple devices—becomes a highly personalized companion, anticipating needs and seamlessly blending into every aspect of users' lives.

In essence, Apple Intelligence is a transformative layer of technology that enhances the MacBook Pro's functionality, making it more than just a powerful device. By embedding machine learning and AI directly into its hardware, Apple has opened new avenues for creating a truly responsive, intuitive computing experience that evolves with the user. This is just the beginning of what could be an era of increasingly intelligent Apple devices, paving the way for a future where our technology learns, adapts, and grows alongside us, redefining the possibilities of personal computing.

Chapter 10: Recommendations and Buying Guide

Choosing the right MacBook Pro with the M4 series comes down to a blend of personal needs, budget, and anticipated workload. Each model within the M4 lineup—the base M4, the M4 Pro, and the M4 Max—has been crafted to serve distinct types of users, offering varying degrees of performance, memory, and storage options that cater to different professional and personal needs. Understanding which configuration aligns with your usage can help make the investment worthwhile, ensuring that your MacBook Pro becomes a tool that complements and enhances your day-to-day workflow.

For most users, the base M4 model is an excellent choice, offering robust power for tasks like document editing, web browsing, video calls, and moderate creative work. With 16 GB of memory and 512 GB of storage standard, this model provides a balance of power and price that suits general users, students, and professionals who require reliable performance without necessarily needing top-tier graphics or intensive computing power. On the other hand, the M4 Pro elevates capabilities for those who work with demanding software, including 4K video editing, design tools, and heavy multitasking. Its higher memory options and enhanced processing power make it suitable for professionals who need a bit more from their machine without investing in maximum configurations.

For users with highly specialized needs, the M4 Max offers unmatched power and storage capacity. This model is ideal for creative professionals in fields like 3D animation, software development, high-resolution video production, and data analysis, where real-time rendering and rapid processing are essential. With up to 128 GB of memory and storage options reaching 8 TB, the M4 Max is an investment in maximum productivity and performance, supporting complex workflows that demand both speed and reliability.

For those considering a MacBook Air as an alternative, the decision often boils down to weighing power against portability and price. The MacBook Air, equipped with the M2 or M3 chips, is a lightweight, more affordable option suited to users who primarily engage in lighter tasks and prioritize mobility. While the Air lacks the sheer power and features of the Pro models, it remains a highly capable machine, ideal for students, frequent travelers, or those seeking a device for general use. The Pro, by contrast, caters to users needing higher processing power, more memory, and improved graphics capabilities—particularly valuable in professional or creative settings.

Before making a purchase, it's essential to consider key factors like configuration, storage, and budget. Think about your typical tasks and assess whether the base model M4 can handle them or if you'd benefit from the added capabilities of the M4 Pro or Max. Additionally, consider future-proofing your investment; opting for slightly higher memory or storage can extend the MacBook's usefulness over time, especially as applications become more resource-intensive. Budget is also an important factor; while the M4 Max offers incredible power, the cost may only be justifiable for users who can utilize its full capabilities. For most, the M4 or M4 Pro strikes a solid balance of price and performance.

In summary, the M4 MacBook Pro lineup offers configurations for nearly every need, from everyday users to top-tier professionals. By aligning your choice with your specific requirements, workflow, and budget, you can ensure that your MacBook Pro will serve as a powerful, lasting tool, ready to support and grow with you as your needs evolve. With its range of configurations and powerful capabilities, the M4 series proves once again that the MacBook Pro is designed to meet and exceed the demands of modern computing, making it a worthy choice for any user.

Conclusion

Reflecting on the journey of the MacBook Pro, it's clear that this laptop represents much more than just a tool—it's a testament to Apple's dedication to innovation, performance, and user experience. This book has explored each aspect of the M4 series MacBook Pro, from its powerful M4 chip family and Nano-Texture display to its enhanced battery life, connectivity options, camera features, and intelligence capabilities. Each detail embodies Apple's meticulous approach to crafting a device that not only meets but anticipates the needs of its users, balancing advanced technology with elegance and usability. The journey from the early Intel-based models to today's powerful M4 series is a story of steady evolution, where Apple has consistently pushed the boundaries of performance, design, and seamless integration, redefining what a laptop can achieve.

As the MacBook Pro continues to evolve, we can only imagine what the future holds. Apple's commitment to in-house silicon has opened new possibilities for advancements in speed, graphics, and energy efficiency, with each new chip iteration bringing the MacBook Pro closer to unprecedented levels of performance. Future models might integrate even more sophisticated AI and machine learning capabilities, pushing the boundaries of personalized computing and intelligent task management. Potential developments in display technology, such as OLED or higher refresh rates, could enhance visuals further, while advancements in battery technology could make all-day use even more accessible. Apple's track record suggests they will continue to improve connectivity options, expand configurations, and refine designs to maintain the MacBook Pro's standing as a powerful yet user-centric machine.

In conclusion, the MacBook Pro's story reflects Apple's enduring impact on the laptop industry and its vision for the future. Each update, from chips to displays to AI integration, signifies Apple's commitment to pushing technological boundaries while staying true to its core philosophy: creating devices that elevate the user experience. As Apple shapes the landscape of computing, the MacBook Pro stands as a powerful example of what's possible when technology and vision come together. For the creative professional, the tech enthusiast, and the everyday user, the MacBook Pro remains a reliable, powerful companion, built to support the demands of today while paving the way for tomorrow.

www.ingramcontent.com/pod-product-compliance
Lightning Source LLC
LaVergne TN
LVHW012346240425
809567LV00009B/408